PHOTO CREDITS

Front Cover & 1 – stephan kerkhofs, 3DMI. 2 – ValSN. 3 – Eric Isselee, Tiplyashina Evgeniya, ictor Jiang. 4 – Tatiana Katsai, Syda Productions, Lopolov. 5 – Flamingo Images, Aila Images, digitalskillet. 6 – Eric Isselee. 7 – Pedro Gutierrez. 8 – Nina Buday. 9 – Tiplyashina Evgeniya. 10 – Helga Yastrebova23, art nick. 11 – Jackie Neff. 12 – Zenobillis. 13 – ThamKC. 14 – Master1305. 15 – ValSN. 16 – wavebreakmedia. 17 – Africa Studio, BIGANDT.COM, Victor Jiang, Pandas. 18 & 19 – Sascha Christian, chaoss, Masarik, Richard Chaff. 20 – Cavan-Images. 21 – mantinov. 22 & 23 – Eric Isselee. Images are courtesy of Shutterstock.com, with thanks to Getty Images, Thinkstock Photo, and iStockphoto.

Words that look like **this** can be found in the glossary on page 24.

Published in 2022 by
KidHaven Publishing, an Imprint of Greenhaven Publishing, LLC
29 E. 21st Street
New York, NY 10010

© 2022 Booklife Publishing
This edition is published by arrangement with Booklife Publishing

All rights reserved. No part of this book may be reproduced in any form without permission in writing from the publisher, except by a reviewer.

Edited by: Shalini Vallepur
Designed by: Lydia Williams

Cataloging-in-Publication Data

Names: Holmes, Kristy.
Title: Life cycle of a dog / Kristy Holmes.
Description: New York : KidHaven Publishing, 2022. | Series: Life cycles | Includes glossary and index.
Identifiers: ISBN 9781534539945 (pbk.) | ISBN 9781534539969 (library bound) | ISBN 9781534539952 (6 pack) | ISBN 9781534539976 (ebook)
Subjects: LCSH: Dogs--Life cycles--Juvenile literature.
Classification: LCC SF426.5 H654 2022 | DDC 599.77'2156--dc23

Printed in the United States of America

CPSIA compliance information: Batch #CWKH22: For further information contact Greenhaven Publishing LLC, New York, New York at 1-844-317-7404.

Please visit our website, www.greenhavenpublishing.com. For a free color catalog of all our high-quality books, call toll free 1-844-317-7404 or fax 1-844-317-7405.

CONTENTS

Page 4	**What Is a Life Cycle?**
Page 6	**Darling Dogs**
Page 8	**Paw-fect Pregnancy**
Page 10	**Precious Puppies**
Page 12	**Jumping Juveniles**
Page 14	**Delightful Dogs!**
Page 16	**Life as a Dog**
Page 18	**Fun Facts About Dogs**
Page 20	**The End of Life as a Dog**
Page 22	**The Life Cycle**
Page 24	**Glossary and Index**

WHAT IS A LIFE CYCLE?

All living things have a life cycle. They are born, they grow bigger, and their bodies change.

Baby

Child

Toddler

When they are fully grown, they have **offspring** of their own. In the end, all living things die. This is the life cycle.

DARLING DOGS

Dogs are **mammals**. They have four legs and a tail. Most dogs are covered in fur. Dogs have wet noses and pads on their feet, or paws.

Fur

Wet Nose

Tail

Paws

Claws

Dogs can smell things from very far away.

Different breeds are good at different things.

Pomeranian

Doberman Pinscher

Dogs are **domestic** animals. This means they can live with humans. Dogs come in all shapes and sizes. These different types are called breeds.

PAW-FECT PREGNANCY

A mother dog carries her babies in her belly before they are born. This is called pregnancy. Dogs are pregnant for around 63 days.

Can you see this mother's **swollen** belly?

A group of puppies born to the same mother at the same time is called a litter.

Some dog breeds only have one or two babies, or puppies, at a time. Other breeds can have as many as 10 puppies at once!

PRECIOUS PUPPIES

Puppies are born with their eyes and ears closed. This means they cannot see or hear. They stay with their mother to keep warm.

By the time they are a few weeks old, their eyes and ears open. They can stand and run around. They love to play!

JUMPING JUVENILES

By the time they are six months old, puppies are bigger, and some may look like their parents. Their fur often grows too.

This is called the juvenile stage. At this age, young dogs grow very quickly, and they soon reach their adult size.

Puppies learn about the world around them by exploring, playing, smelling, and licking.

DELIGHTFUL DOGS!

When the puppy is fully grown, it is an adult dog. Adult dogs all look different. Dogs can look like one of their parents or a mixture of the two.

Adult dogs are ready to find a **mate** and have babies of their own. Female dogs will look after their puppies as they grow.

This mother is playing with her baby.

LIFE AS A DOG

Do you have a pet dog?

Dogs eat mostly meat, but they can eat some fruits and vegetables too. Most dogs live with humans.

Some dogs are working dogs. Dogs are very clever and can do a lot of different jobs to help people.

Herding Dog

Rescue Dog

Police Dog

Service Dog

FUN FACTS ABOUT DOGS

A dog's noseprint is **unique** – just like a human fingerprint!

Most adult dogs have 42 teeth.

Dogs hang their tongues out and **pant** to cool down.

Some dog breeds have no fur or hair! Others may have only a little hair on their head or tail.

THE END OF LIFE AS A DOG

Some dogs get gray hairs as they get older – just like people do.

Dogs live for around 7 to 15 years, but this might be longer or shorter depending on the breed.

Dogs slow down as they get older, and you might need to be gentler and quieter around them. Older dogs might sleep more and like to snuggle. Some might prefer to be left alone.

THE LIFE CYCLE

A dog's life cycle has different stages. Each stage looks different from the last.

Juvenile

Adult Dog

A puppy is born with its eyes and ears closed. A juvenile grows into an adult dog, and then the adult dog has offspring of its own.

In the end, the dog dies, and the life cycle is complete.

GLOSSARY

domestic — when an animal is tame and can be kept by humans

mammals — animals that are warm-blooded, have a backbone, and make milk to feed their young

mate — a partner (of the same species) that an animal chooses to have babies with

offspring — the babies of an animal or plant

pant — to take short, quick breaths

swollen — larger than normal

unique — unlike anything or anyone else

INDEX

babies 4, 8, 15
breeds 7, 9, 20
fur 6, 12

hearing 10
litters 9
play 11, 13, 15

puppies 9–10, 12–15, 22–23
smell 6, 13